# Kinky Keeps the House Clean

**Mari Deweese**

Nixes Mate Books
Allston, Massachusetts

Copyright © 2017 Mari Deweese

Book design by d'Entremont
Cover photo from the collection of Lauren Leja

All rights reserved. This book or any portion thereof may not be reproduced or used in any manner whatsoever without the express written permission of the publisher except for the use of brief quotations in a book review or scholarly journal.

Some of these poems appeared in *Pressure Press Presents*, *Chickenshit Bingo* and *The Wingnut Brigade*.

Special thanks to: Michael McInnis (because it was his idea in the first place), Ron Androla (for seconding that motion), and Mike Roach (for staying on my ass about getting a book out) – I'd say stay kinky, but I don't think that's ever gonna be an issue for y'all. Also, black tea – I'd be lost without you.

ISBN 978-0-692-83008-6

Nixes Mate Books
POBox 1179
Allston, MA 02134
nixesmate.pub/books

I'll be as dirty as I please, and I like to be dirty, and I will be dirty!

> Emily Brontë, *Wuthering Heights*

# Kinky Keeps the House Clean

**Kinky Needs**

I am not robustly prone to anal-anything, but I will fantasize so hard about fucking your ass up if you argue that there's no wrong way to load a dishwasher.

Mix my body up
stir it, cure it til it leaks
from your rock-hardness.

The only possible reason I would even consider making up this bed is if it might tempt you later to break it, or me on it.

His lust shadows her the way a pack and a half of generic Dramamine does: with men of sticks creeping down the road to show her the water that's really concrete; laughing faces that melt and run down her bare arms to congregate between her legs as an insidious puddle; a single electrical box running faster than the cars moving on the street, under frenzied lamps, running and screaming in terror that spins the vortex of the reactor inside her filmy pleasure cells bursting with delirium.

A wet brown ring on the counter from the mug hot in my hand reminds me, I need to wash that towel and the sheets from our bed as soon as I finish my tea.

I have seen
what love without
a resting place
becomes: dark wings
searching for some
sign of life, flying
alone above the flood.

**Kinky Muses**

It is only now, in the silent aftermath of our taking and leavings, that I hear how the fire alarm in the hallway softly, sporadically beeps a low-battery warning and recollect that we are out of double A's.

I don't make castles out of sand.
I do make dicks out of brains.

Fuck me like you mean it.
I mean it like you fuck.

Oh! this shitty erotica, it's not ART!
Art IS shitty – this is not erotica. OH!

Kinky in the bathroom, ass up on the sink-
sounds just like a nursery rhyme,
good rhythm, dontcha think?

He groans, FUUAAGGHH, she shatters
and screams: I FUCK MYSELF BETTER,
I JUST DO THIS FOR THE T-SHIRT!

Sweet cheese & crackers, if you come up from behind and interrupt me cooking one more time, I might just make you get it up, get it in, and then I'll really get a facial from draining the pasta.

In a pipette squeeze
of semen swims galaxies
whitewasted, redholed

It's an ironic satisfaction, I suppose, that the cock you can't aim gets to make my ass shake while I'm vigorously scrubbing your piss off the porcelain.

You can't make me,
you won't
make me fall in love.
That is all the preface
you will get.

I know. I know the way
a breath turns into
bubbles, becomes laughter
in the bloodstream
of the golden sort, a bell
singing over hills, lava
bursting through blackened
cracks, unrepentant
in downward resolution
burning slowly, vegetation
catching fire.

And if you made me
coffee and brought me breakfast
in bed, I'd glow,
I'll admit it, all
cozy-fluttery, sheepish smile,
sleep-pink lips upon you
shining. Then I'd think,

why is the fan off?
and kick
out of the blanket nest
I'd built
cuz it's too stifling
to even fucking breathe.

**Kinky Questions**

Hanging down the stairs, anchored by my elbows gripping the step I am facing, I wonder if you ever notice how lint-free I maintain the crease at each rise, because I certainly don't.

When people in love stare into each other's eyes, their heartbeats sync together.

(I just read it on Pinterest, so it must be true.)

I sold my soul for a lonely boy. I think I might have let him swallow my shyness with his eyes, while I blushed and tried to stay still during the ocular invasion. I was considerably less shy about the pictures he kept on his Nokia, though they were devoured just as easily. But I never heard our hearts in tandem.

(There was a girl once. She didn't like to look in someone's eyes either, and we weren't in love, but I swear, in the frenzied way we groped each other on the dead playground, pressing in hard, tongues sparking like flint in our mouths that combusted into silver filaments of spider silk, entangled, sticky, hot inhales becoming one on exhale, I think what if that means our heart beats synced up, too?)

I'll never know, now.

I swear, if you liked me on my knees half as much as you blather about, you'd let me get back to cleaning these gross-ass grout lines.

Island I am not.
Presently peninsular,
and sea levels rise.

The lights have all been shut off, the doors locked for the night, and I wonder if you're taking a shit while you beat off to the taboo porn on your phone, or if you are saving any electricity for me.

**Kinky Confessions**

A rage of flame becomes
a higher hell
than all the paradise
of proffered grace.
Against the gateless pearl
need exacts a greater price,
erases what sanctity
has held too long
with loveless arms.
No need for pursuit
to mount the wall.
The blood pulses. The strong
hot scent of violence
permeates the space
by way of putrescent
blossoms in their urn.
A trigger on the finger
blows a middle
kiss to signal the armies it is
time to burn celestial,
time to feed the abyss.
But this flame of mine will eat
even after
my womb
has gorged on
dead men's lastlaughter.

You holler at me from inside to light the grill while I'm out here sweeping the patio, so I do, and stub the match out on the compass I inked with a safety pin on the inside of my ankle, breathing sharply through my nose as Kegels clench.

'Course I believe
in resurreXion. I've died
and risen plenty.

Sunday after-church handjobs have certainly improved my stamina for enduring the mundane, a skill I find immensely useful for tasks such as polishing chair rails and dusting each individual slat of the window blinds.

Bless me, Father, for I have sinned. On Tuesday last, I snorted 2 lines of something called Shanghai Girl, and let a clique of gangbangers use my body in a most unholy fashion. I also accepted monetary compensation for my iniquitous actions, so I could pay \*\*\*'s bill at the after-hours clinic. He thinks I was at the bookstore, because I told a lie, and feel rather guilty about that.

**Kinky Twists**

I found this stiff g-string wadded up in the side pocket of your jeans, so now, after vacuuming the living room carpet, I fuck the floor while I grip the memento in my fist, coming hard to the thought of her coming all over you.

What are these breasts
but anger
and sadness
unearthed? I rip them off
and eat them
till my stomach turns
and I spew forth
the rancidity.

My mouth is bitter
with foul things. My tongue
crouches in its own
excrement.

And down my throat:
vines
and broken witches'
fingers claw
all voice and breath
away.

With the hose gripped tightly in my hand, I watch the neighbor-from-down-the-street's shirtless son drip sweat while he mows his front lawn, and I imagine this long green tube wrapped twice around my neck, water scalding our faded blue hydrangeas.

The smallness of your lips
enveloped by the hunger
mine have didn't stop me
from trying to swallow you.
    Little man, with your small

    appetite that at last killed
    mine. So fuck you. There
will never be
a ravenosity
    as hard as my love
    with only air to eat.

Before I get back to fixing the loose hinges on the bathroom cabinet, I smush the fingerprint bruises on my inner thigh, and smile at the sharpness of the screwdriver in my skin.

# Kinky Dreams

I'll say, I don't want
to hurt you.

(Maybe.) All
I really want is
to actually feel the wind

coming down
from purple hull
hills on muted days

of only grey,
to see as much
of green as my eyes are

able to gulp,
as much of blue
as my bones are shaded.

But I do not need you
for any of that.

Catching my reflection in the bay window, I make note of smudges in need of Windex, vague shapes of leftover epithethelials and oil: a right hand, a belly button, a pair of tits, the left only a partial print, a waning gibbous moon staring out from the pane.

I dreamt of you again last night.

I hate you for visiting, for interrupting the Nothing At All that fills my head on nearly every night. I don't ever dream anymore. And I am glad for it. Except, that I did last night and you were there.

The first time you came as a demon with eyes the color of the palest blue that lies behind strands of Cirrus; I was mesmerized, and you moved me in my secret place I've never shared with any man, and gave me a skeleton key to something important I never could remember. And when the other devils came you left me on the mountain where they could not come and told me we would meet again, your eyes burning into my brain, and I woke with a wet face, sobbing into my sheets.

A year later you came as something in the water while I slept. Fearing nothing I stood on cliff's edge and watched the white and black waves smash against the rocks so far below me. Then, a shock like a gut punch, as I saw a face in the water that I'd never seen but knew was you, and I jumped. Needles of cold punctured my body, but I was on fire, desperate to find you, and in the darkness I felt you, though I could not see. Your mouth found mine, and I plummeted, deeper than the depth of the sea. Suddenly I found myself thrown back to shore, soaked, chilled. I searched the horizon for you again, and I waited there, shaking, until my body finally demanded release and I regained consciousness. This time, my face was dry, but I had thrown off the covers and lay in a circle of sweat, despite the fan above me.

The last time you came to me was ten years ago, and you pulled me into the shadow of a cave as I walked along a beach path. I was frightened until I saw your eyes, and then I knew you had found me again. All I wanted was to melt into you, aware as I was that we existed only in dreams, so that I never had to wake without you. But we could not merge. The universe inside my head did not allow it and we both cried, and watched as the night began to fade and the light over the water grew, knowing our time would be over soon. This time, when I opened my eyes, I felt only emptiness, eating the fear.

I was young then. I still dreamed. I was still wide-eyes behind blue steel. But now I am this. And you come to me, like this, when I do not go to sleep to dream and what is wide inside me is a pit where things go to die.

I will not forgive you for leaving this time. In whatever universe that you exist apart from me, I hope you wake in hell.

I shut my eyes:

sleek under my hand, cool wood
of the rail I rest against becomes
the dermal taste of your back
my fingers uncurl and drink
as if you were Liatris aspera
and they, ten ravenous
butterfly tongues;

inside the spaces between the strands
of my hair whisper visible sounds,
the waves on the inside
of my skull like so many scrawling
words imbedded
red in aural bone;

into the empty air ahead I lean
and catch a glimmer from the face
of other emptiness, glints
that have reflected too many times
off too many clouds and other
harder surfaces to hold
enough of light to do me
any good this evening.

I open my eyes:

tiptoes push weight up as heels rise,
balance shifts forward, and over
I fall.

I kiss you while you sleep, my lips pillowing a subtle suction against the slippery brace of my tongue, and your top lip is like the dirty plate I just washed in the sink, round, smooth, lathered in my hands, waterwrinkled fingers sliding through effervescent lemon.

**Kinky Rises**

I am leaving you my least favorite bra, the one you like me to wear, the ring I bought my own damn self, and the recipe for my grandmother's lamb stew, because I'm allowed to be kind, but everything else I am burning in the barrels out back before I go.

If I've never read all the writers I am supposed to have read by now does that make me a fake or an original? Scratch of graphite, brush stroke, bristles, turpentine song to me sounds like worms moving through and eating earth, rebirthing darkness in the bowels as something that is not quite, but leads to, life. And here I muse a little space, about six inches worth, at the maiden in the bow of my brain, dead for years and still floating on the river of untersee current, imagining if she'd still live, had I read all the writers I was supposed to have read, or if I'd be dead by now, too.

I see now that blue squills and daffodils are enough to cut the string that has held this broken kite to earth for too long, and today, I am lovely.

I don't need to be clean.

## About the Author

Mari Deweese lives outside of Memphis, and dreams of a place with an actual autumn. When she is not busy with that and other similarly useless pursuits, she is probably writing, thinking about writing, or cleaning the kitchen.

Nixes Mate is a tiny island in Boston Harbor first used by colonists to graze their sheep. The island became infamous after the bodies of convicted pirates were gibbetted there to serve as warnings to mutinous sailors.

Nixes Mate Books features small-batch artisanal literature, created by writers that use all 26 letters of the alphabet and then some, honing their craft the time-honored way: one line at a time.

**More Nixes Mate titles:**
On Broad Sound | Rusty Barnes

**Forthcoming titles from Nixes Mate:**
Squall Line on the Horizon | Pris Campbell
Hitchhiking Beatitudes | Michael McInnis
Lubbock Electric | Anne Elezabeth Pluto
Comes to This | Jeff Weddle
Nixes Mate Review Anthology 2016/17
Stories | Lauren Leja

nixesmate.pub/books

www.ingramcontent.com/pod-product-compliance
Lightning Source LLC
Chambersburg PA
CBHW051957290426
44110CB00015B/2284